Status of Adivasis/Indigenous Peoples Mining Series – 4

MEGHALAYA

Status of Adivasis/Indigenous Peoples Mining Series – 4

MEGHALAYA

Gideon L Kharkongor and Rajesh Dutta

Status of Adivasis/Indigenous Peoples Mining Series – 4 :
MEGHALAYA

Gideon L Kharkongor and Rajesh Dutta

First Published, 2014

ISBN 978-93-5002-284-9

Published by
AAKAR BOOKS
28 E Pocket IV, Mayur Vihar Phase I, Delhi 110 091
Phone: 011 2279 5505 Telefax: 011 2279 5641
aakarbooks@gmail.com; www.aakarbooks.com

In association with
THE OTHER MEDIA
J 139, First Floor, Vikas Puri
New Delhi 110 018
Phones: 011 2854 3372/73, Fax: 011 4237 1129
Email: tom@theothermedia.org

Printed at
Saurabh Printers Pvt. Ltd., A 16, Sector IV, Noida

Acknowledgements

The Status of Adivasis/Indigenous Peoples (SAIP) has been an important initiative of The Other Media and All India Coordinating Forum of Adivasis/Indigenous Peoples. It began with a lot of interest and enthusiasm with a wide consultation among activists, scholars and researchers interested in Adivasis/Indigenous People's issues. However, the process seemed to have had its own pace and could not keep up with the expectation of completing the report on tome. The present phase of the programme has covered, state-wise, issues of land and mining in the Adivasis/Indigenous People's areas.

This report on mining issues in the Adivasi areas of Meghalaya has been prepared by Gideon L Kharkongor and Rajesh Dutta. Members of the EC went through the report and gave their valuable comments and suggestions. We gratefully acknowledge their contribution that was available at every stage of preparation of the report. The efforts of the EC have been untiringly coordinated by C R Bijoy. The reports owe a lot to his relentless efforts to keep in the loop everyone concerned towards producing good results out of the reports. At the level of The Other Media, Ravi Hemadri, who worked as the Executive Director of the organisation through most part of the programme serves as a link between the organisation and the EC. He continued to coordinate the final editing and printing of the reports. We gratefully acknowledge the role played by both C R Bijoy and Ravi Hemadri.

We acknowledge and thank the Adivasi Academy, Tejgarh, Gujarat, and particularly Prof Ganesh Devy, for generously hosting in February 2008, a two-day workshop of members of the EC and authors to review the draft reports. We thank the members of the Advisory Board of the SAIP, who with their participation in the first consultation and later whenever called upon, gave their inputs to the reports. Thanks are due to Shankar Gopalakrishnan who meticulously put together statistical data and selected literature for SAIP.

Finally we would like to acknowledge and thank our funders ICCO, Netherlands, and TROCAIRE, Ireland, who supported the programme right through the last five years. We are grateful to the Foundation for Ecological Security, Anand, Gujarat, and OXFAM who generously supported the printing of the first phase of reports on land. We thank all of them for being patient with this initiative.

E Deenadayalan
General Secretary

Contents

List of Tables

Acronyms and Abbreviations

AEC	Atomic Energy Commission
AMD	Atomic Mineral Department
BARC	Bhabha Atomic Research Centre
C&RD Blocks	Community and Rural Development Blocks
CAMPA	Compensatory Afforestation Fund Management and Planning Authority
CCAUM	Coordination Committee Against Uranium Mining
CCEA	Cabinet Committee on Economic Affairs
CMCL	Cement Manufacturing Company Limited
CMD	Chairman-cum-Managing Director
DAE	Department of Atomic Energy
DE	Directory Enterprise
DMO	Divisional Mining Officer
DMR	Directorate of Mineral Resources
DPR	Detailed Project Report
DTH	Direct-to-Home
EIA	Environment Impact Assessment
EMP	Environment Management Plan
EPIP	Export Promotion Industrial Park
GSI	Geological Survey of India
HESPO	Hynñiewtrep Environment Status Preservation Organisation
HNLC	Hynñiewtrep National Liberation Council
IFC	International Foreign Corporation

IIT	Indian Institute of Technology
JIT	Joint Inspection Team
KHADC	Khasi Autonomous District Hills Council
KSU	Khasi Students Union
LUMPL	Lafarge Umiam Mining Pvt. Ltd.
LWLDO	Langrin War-San Lyngdoh Development Organisation
LYWO	Lai Lyngdoh Welfare Organisation
MAA	Meghalaya Adventure Association
MLA	Member of Legislative Assembly
MMDR	Mines and Minerals (Development and Regulation) Act 1957
MPCB	Meghalaya State Pollution Control Board
MPHRC	Meghalaya People's Human Rights Council
MT	Metric Tonnes
NDE	Non-Directory Enterprise
NGO	Non-Governmental Organisations
NOC	No Objection Certificate
NSDP	Net State Domestic Product
OAE	Own Account Enterprise
PIL	Public Interest Litigation
SAC	Shella Action Committee
Tpd	Tonnes-per-day
UCIL	Uranium Corporation of India Limited
WYWO	Western Youth Welfare Organisation

Preface

Eighty-eight million Adivasis and indigenous peoples live in India—approximately one-fourth of the world's total indigenous population. Historically self-sufficient, forest-based communities with independent cultural identities, they have been subjected to displacement, dispossession and repression for more than a century and are now India's poorest and most marginalised communities. Since the onset of British rule, and in many cases from much earlier, Adivasis and indigenous peoples have been systematically and forcibly dispossessed of the resources of their homelands. In gross violation of democratic practice, social justice and both constitutional and legal requirements, such dispossession continues to this day. It is also the Adivasis and indigenous peoples who have paid the heaviest price for the current neo-liberal globalisation policies, with their land, resources and forests taken from them for private capital—in the name of 'economic growth'.

These larger processes have been accompanied by the erosion and undermining of cultural identities, leading to a loss of cultural moorings and other markers of ethnicity. Less than half of India's Adivasi communities speak their own language. State and private efforts at 'mainstreaming' and against indigenous faiths, practices and cultural mores have had a devastating impact.

Such trends have not gone unchallenged. Despite

growing differentiation, ethnicity has emerged as a strong, consolidating force. Many have organised, often with the help of sympathetic outsiders, to fight against their oppressors and struggle for the control over land and other resources, and for local self-government as in parts of central India. There have been demands for political self-determination and autonomy of varying degrees as in Jharkhand and the northeast. The state characterises all such struggles as 'Law and Order Problems', and large parts of central India and the northeast are heavily militarised in the name of 'national security'. In other parts too state repression has been heavy and brutal.

Though these processes are well-known to many and particularly to Adivasis and indigenous people's movements, there continues to be a dearth of knowledge on the overall status of Adivasis and indigenous peoples in India. The struggle-based mass organisations of Adivasis and indigenous peoples in the Indian subcontinent articulated the need to work towards such a task in the late 1990s. The collective process to fulfil this task was launched in 2005.

The Status of Adivasis/Indigenous Peoples is conceptualised as a series of reports on salient themes affecting the lives of Adivasis/Indigenous Peoples. In the first instance, the series focuses on the situation of land and mining in the tribal tracts of the country. We hope that the series will be effective in not only deliberating upon similar themes of importance to the Adivasi present and future, but also help strengthening linkages amongst movements, activists, scholars and all others who are concerned with the protection of the rights of Adivasis/Indigenous Peoples in the Indian subcontinent.

This series of reports will explore the history, the laws, and the facts, and describe struggles while providing an overview of current realities. The main purpose of these reports is to expand linkages and relationships between movements, scholars, and activists so that the future of the political struggles is informed and forward looking.

Executive Summary

Meghalaya, by far, is currently the most mined state amongst the northeastern states of India. The State is overwhelmingly tribal-dominated. Known for large deposits of coal and limestone, Jaintia Hills is the most mined area for long. The State is known to have a large deposit of uranium whose mining has been opposed. Largely unregulated, mining has been carried out unscientifically, adversely affecting life, livelihoods, environment and health of the people. This is starkly evident in Jaintia Hills. In contrast to other states with large-scale mining, Meghalaya's land holding pattern is dominated by community ownership unlike the central Indian States, enjoyed by the different tribes according to their specific customs and traditions. This further contributes to the rising conflict around land use and issues of tribal customary claims and ancestral domain.

1

Introduction

This study is an attempt to familiarise the reader with trends in mining in Meghalaya, and the mining of coal in Jaintia Hills in particular. Meghalaya occupies an important place in the mineral map of India. Mining of different minerals from within the State has benefited a large number of industrial activities outside the State, but only a few indigenous industries and people within. The central concern earlier was ensuring value addition and domestic utilisation, but with the passage of time, other serious apprehensions have emerged. Some of these have been raised in subsequent sections. The recent sprout of industrial activities has put greater strain and stress on the environment. The quality of air and water has significantly altered. Changing demographic profiles in the mining areas are evident. An attempt is made to put forth some major areas of anxiety with the intention of impressing upon policy makers to implement suitable policies to ensure a harmonious relationship and balance between economic progress, sustainable economic development and preservation of the environment.

2

Background of Meghalaya

2.1 Area and Location

Meghalaya was created as an Autonomous State within the State of Assam on April 2, 1970 with the two erstwhile Districts of Assam, viz. the United Khasi and Jaintia Hills District and the Garo Hills District. The Autonomous State was upgraded into a full-fledged State on January 21, 1972 with Shillong as its capital. The State has a geographical area of 22,429 sq. kms. and is subdivided into 11 Districts, viz. (i) East Khasi Hills District (ii) West Khasi Hills District (iii) Jaintia Hills District (iv) Ri-Bhoi District (v) West Garo Hills District (vi) East Garo Hills District and (vii) South Garo Hills District (viii) East Jaintia Hills (ix) South West Khasi Hills (x) South West Garo Hills and (xi) North Garo Hills District. At the beginning, the State had 24 Community and Rural Development (C&RD) Blocks, but the number increased to 39 by the end of 2001-2002. It is one of the smallest states in India and is strategically located in the northeast between 25° 5" and 26° 10" north latitudes and between 98° 47′ and 97° 47′ east longitudes. It is a strip of land spread along the northern boundary of Bangladesh and is bounded by that country on the south as well as on the west. The length of the international boundary is about 423 kms. The State is surrounded on the other sides by Assam that provides the access to it mainly by road. The land surface of the State is mostly comprised of hills and table lands with the hills sloping gently towards Assam on the north but rather steeply and abruptly towards Bangladesh on the south.

2.2 Population

According to the 2011 census the total population of the State was 29,66,889 as compared to 23,18,822 in 2001 and 17,74,778 in 1991, indicating a high decadal growth of 27.95 per cent and 29.94 per cent respectively in the last two decades. The reported population density was 103 per square kilometre in 2001 increasing to 132 in 2011. The estimated sex-ratio in 2008 is 988 females per thousand males declining to 989 in 2011. The literacy rate increased from 29.49 per cent in 1971 to 63.31 per cent by 2001 and to 74.43 per cent in 2011, but ranks 17th at the all India level. The rural population accounts for 79.93 per cent, and 20.07 per cent reside in urban areas. The number of towns in Meghalaya has grown from 3 in 1971 to 9 by 2001 with 1 urban agglomeration. The population is pre-dominantly tribal and constitutes 86.15 per cent (2011) of the total population.

The economic classification of population as per the 2001 Population Census revealed that the total workers were 41.8 per cent of the total population and of this 32.6 per cent were main workers and 9.2 per cent marginal workers. Meghalaya being primarily agrarian, cultivators constituted 48.14 per cent of the total workers and 50.2 per cent of main workers. Of the total workers, 17.7 per cent were agricultural labourers, 2.2 per cent were household workers and other workers 31.98 per cent. No separate data of workers in different mining activities such as coal and limestone and allied activities are available.

Table 1 provides a district-wise population break-up. The West Khasi Hills district is the largest in terms of area but also the most underdeveloped; while East Khasi Hills is relatively more developed and populated since the State's capital, Shillong, is located here. East Khasi Hills naturally has the highest population density amongst all districts.

Table 1: District-wise Population of Meghalaya in 2011

Sl. No.	*District*	*Headquarters*	*Area Sq. Kms.*	*Population (2001 Census)*	*Population Density (Persons per Sq. Km.)*
1	East Khasi Hills	Shillong	2,748	825,922	301
2	West Khasi Hills	Nongstoin	5,247	383,461	73
3	Jaintia Hills	Jowai	3,819	395,124	103
4	Ri-Bhoi	Nongpoh	2,448	258,840	106
5	West Garo Hills	Tura	3,714	643,291	175
6	East Garo Hills	Williamnagar	2,603	317,917	122
7	South Garo Hills	Baghmara	1,850	142,334	75
8	**Total**		**22,429**	**2,966,889**	**132**

Source: http://www.census2011.co.in/census/state/districtlist/meghalaya.html

2.3 Soil and Rainfall

The soil in the State is acidic in nature and comparatively rich in organic matter and nitrogen, but poor in phosphorous. Due to heavy rainfall, the soils in the border areas tend to be sandy. The Mawsynram, Cherrapunjee and Pynursla belt in Khasi Hills, along the southern border, records rainfall varying between 1,000 mm to 15,000 mm per year. Large-scale deforestation has exposed the hills to natural vagaries that have caused large-scale erosion of the topsoil and a huge amount of soil being washed away every year. This also led to poor water retention, reduced soil fertility and other problems.

1.1.4 NSDP

The Net State Domestic Product of the State at current prices increased from Rs. 2,165.96 crores in 1997-98 to Rs. 4,754.15 crores in 2004-05 and the corresponding per capita income increased from Rs. 10,270 in 1997-98 to Rs. 19,572 in 2004-05. The NSDP of the State at constant (1993-94) prices was Rs. 1,662.15 crores during 1997-98 and increased to Rs. 2,739.50 crores during 2004-05. The per capita income

(NSDP) at constant (1993-94) prices during 1997-98 was Rs. 7,881 increased to Rs. 11,278 during 2004-05.[1]

1.1.5 Economic Condition

'Cultivators' and 'agricultural labourers' have a share of 66% in the total workforce of the State. The contribution of the primary sector to the State's NSDP is 33% and is relatively much higher than at the national level. This figure would fall if the contribution of mining and quarrying activities is excluded from the primary sector. The tertiary sector contributes 55% of NSDP. With an increase in population, there has been a corresponding decrease in the availability of land per capita for agricultural purposes. While the land-man ratio is high, settled cultivation is primarily restricted to the valley areas. Jhum cultivation is still practised, but with decreasing cycles. An increasing number of cultivators have led to fragmentation of land. According to the data released by the Department of Agriculture in its Agricultural Census Report, from 1970–71 to 1995-96, the number of operational holdings increased and the average size of operational holdings under all sub-categories decreased.[2] Further, a larger number of agricultural labourers points to both landless labour and poverty. With the secondary sector either decelerating or remaining stagnant, the agricultural sector has had to absorb the surplus labour. As per the 10th Five Year Plan (Draft Proposals), 49% of the populace lived below the poverty line.

The State is plagued by numerous inadequate infrastructural facilities. The hilly terrain is overtly responsible for poor road networking within the State. Many villages are yet to be properly connected. By 2003-04 only 60.19% or 3,301 villages were electrified. Such inadequacies have hampered rapid and even economic growth and progress. Hence, despite possessing a fairly rich resource

1. *Meghalaya Economics and Statistics*, 2006.
2. *Statistical Abstract Meghalaya*, 2006.

base, which logically should have propelled the secondary sector, Meghalaya remains industrially backward.

The State's Industrial Policy of 1997 provided a number of incentives for investments in industrial activities. Subsequently, a number of units were set up at the Export Promotion Industrial Park (EPIP), Byrnihat and in the industrial area of Barapani. However, most of these units, either producing commodities or providing services, do not display strong resources-industry linkages.[3] The secondary sector's contribution to NSDP as per estimates of 2001-02, remained below 13%, and the contribution of the 'manufacturing' sub-sector fell from a high of 39% in 1990-91 to 16% in 2001-02. The share of 'unregistered units' under 'manufacturing' continues to outweigh the registered ones. Hence, it is the sub-sector 'construction' with the largest share of around 80% within the secondary sector. This clearly establishes the weak resource-industry linkage in Meghalaya.

Meghalaya's economy is thus government expenditure dependent and driven, and not market-driven. The backwardness is also explicit from the modes of exploration and exploitation of its natural resources. The export of most unprocessed minerals and other primary products to markets outside the State has prevented the benefits of backward and forward linkages and vertical integration between industrial units.

3. See Dutta, 2005.

3

Tribal Concepts of Resource Control

3.1 Land Tenure

Meghalaya has a unique land holding system that is governed by the Sixth Schedule of the Indian Constitution. There has not been any change in the traditional land holding pattern that has been practised since time immemorial. The land system in Meghalaya is mainly community ownership where government has little or no say at all. The private party leases the land or may sell the land to the government on request or demand. Hence, any activity on the land is purely unorganised and lacks any systematic arrangement or records. Land is not codified but is based mainly on the socio-religious customs and clan monopolisation. Though land ownership is common, yet the occupancy right is individual. Landed property is usually in the custody of the youngest daughter who is called the *Khatduh*. The brothers and the maternal uncle(s) may advise her from time to time on the share and sale of land. Interestingly, the father who is the head of the household, has no part to play in matters concerning land. Private land can be mortgaged, sold, transferred or utilised in any manner. One of the main features of the Khasi land tenure system is the ambiguity surrounding the concept of ownership, control and occupancy right of some categories of land, notably public land, clan land and ancestral land.

Land classification is of two types:

1. Public lands or *Ri Raid*
2. Private lands or *Ri Kynti*

Both these in effect are private lands where government has little or no say at all. While public land is with the clan or community, private on the other hand is with an individual or the family. *Ri Raid* is community land where the village chief is often called by different names in different areas like the *Syiem* (King), *Lyngdohs, Dolois, Myntris, Sirdars, Wahdadars,* etc. The ownership is with everyone belonging to the community. So one can build a house, cultivate or use land without owning it or payment of revenue. Land is free for all as long as it is being utilised in a meaningful way. Most of the forestland belongs to the *Raid* and its products go to the *Raid.* The *Ri Kynti* belongs to the particular clan (*kur*) or family (*iing*) by virtue of inheritance or acquirement. The control and authority is with the *Khatduh* who has the property rights, of use and occupancy. The inherited land (*nongtymmen*) cannot be sold or leased, but can be transferred within the lineage clan.

With the changing times, the clan or the community pays taxes to the Chief or the *Syiem* whenever land is sold, transferred or mortgaged. Though, land cannot be sold to non-tribals, yet instances exist where land has been sold to non-tribals.

3.2 Meghalaya Transfer of Land (Regulation) Act

In 1948 the Government of Assam framed the following rules to safeguard the indigenous land:

> No land belonging to a Khasi shall be sold, bartered, leased, given or otherwise transferred or caused to be sold, bartered, mortgaged, leased, given or otherwise transferred to a non-Khasi except with the previous sanction of the provincial government.

In 1953 the United Khasi-Jaintia Hills District Council adopted the United Khasi-Jaintia Hills District Council (Transfer of Land) Act 1953. The salient features of the Act are:

1. No land was to be sold, mortgaged, leased, bartered, gifted or otherwise transferred by a tribal to a non-tribal or by a non-tribal to another non-tribal except with the previous sanction of the District Council.
2. Sanction was not to be accorded to the sale from a tribal to a non-tribal if the intended transferee either already held one piece of house property or land in Shillong, within five miles from the Deputy Commissioner's court, either in his name or in the name of other members of his family or falls within the category of the class of profiteering landlord.
3. A report from the local administrative heads to be received.
4. There was no provision for right of appeal.

In 1971 the newly formed State of Meghalaya passed the Meghalaya Transfer of Land (Regulation) Act 1971, which was subsequently amended four times by the legislature. The salient features of the Act are:

1. The Act is applicable to the tribal areas only.
2. Transfer includes gifts, sale, exchange, mortgage, lease, surrender, or any mode of transfer.
3. No land in Meghalaya shall be transferred by a tribal to a non-tribal or by a non-tribal to another non-tribal except with the previous sanction of the competent authority.
4. The government may, by notification, prohibit the transfer of land within specified areas.
5. In granting or refusing sanction, the competent authority shall consider:

    a) Whether the non-tribal holds any other land in Meghalaya
    b) Whether any tribal is willing to buy the land at market value
    c) Whether the non-tribal is carrying on any business, profession or vocation in or near the area and whether for the purposes of such business,

profession or vocation, it is necessary for him to reside in the area.

d) Whether the proposed transfer is likely to promote the economic interests of Scheduled Tribes in the area.

e) No land belonging to a tribal shall be sold in execution of any decree or order passed by a court or any other authority to any tribal except with the previous permission of the competent authority.

f) Right of appeal is incorporated; the appeal is to the board of revenue, whose order will be final.

There have been attempts to bring a policy change in matters of land holding, but it has not succeeded. The Land Reforms Commission set up in 1973 for looking into matters of land holding and codification of customary land laws have not seen the light of day.

3.3 Forests

The area under forests has remained unchanged at 949.56 thousand ha between 1994 and 2004 as per statistics released by the Principal Chief Conservator of Forests, Meghalaya. This is rather surprising when it is well-known that illegal felling of trees has continued despite the Supreme Court ban. The present Chief Minister declared in the Assembly that in the years 2004-05, 2005-06 and 2006-07, the number of illegal tree felling cases were 110, 79 and 109 respectively. He also stated that of the 188 illegal saw mills, only 140 had been sealed by the Forest Department authorities.[4]

The State Forest Department has under its control about 10% of all forests consisting of Reserve Forests, Protected Forests and National Parks whose respective sizes are 71.27, 1.24 and 26.75 thousand ha. The remaining 850.30 thousand ha or 90% are referred to as 'Unclassed' forests. These forests

4. *The Shillong Times*, May 8, 2008.

managed by the District Councils of Khasi, Jaintia and Garo Hills in their jurisdictions are of three types (i) old unclassed forests directly under their control, (ii) forests owned by clans and communities and (iii) private forests from where Councils collect royalty when timber is exported. The rapid depletion of forests led to afforestation and social forestry programmes during the 7th Plan. These were undertaken in community and private lands through grant-in-aid assistance to the District Councils.

4

Mining and Minerals in the State

The Directorate of Mineral Resources (DMR), Government of Meghalaya which functions under the administrative department of Mining and Geology at the secretariat level is responsible for planning and execution of geological investigations, levy and collection of revenue. The Director is assisted by a team of ministerial and technical staff, stationed at Shillong and by two Divisional Mining Officers (DMOs)—posted at Jowai in Jaintia Hills District and Williamnagar in East Garo Hills District. Thirteen check gates have been set up at various locations in the State. The Geological Survey of India (GSI) too has been involved in the process of exploration and mapping, core drilling and exploratory mining.

The current rates of royalty as fixed by the Government of India (Schedule 2 of Mines and Minerals (Development and Regulation) Act 1957) are: Rs. 165 per tonne for coal, Rs. 45 per tonne for limestone, Rs. 20 per tonne for quartz, and 2.5% of the sale price on ad-valorem basis for Sillimanite.

The major minerals available in the State of Meghalaya are coal, limestone, kaolin (China clay) and small quantities of sillimanite, bauxite, apetite, granite, glass sand, quartz, uranium and others. Large-scale mining takes place in coal and limestone. Uranium has been discovered but not mined, and is a much debated issue in the State. Sillimanite deposits that ranked first in the country years ago have been exhausted due to exploitative mining. The State Government has not given much attention to the sector 'Industry and Minerals' as evident from the approved outlays under different Five Year Plans. From the 6th to the 10th Five Year Plan, the sub-sector of 'Industry and Minerals' received less than 5% of the total outlays.

The estimated district-wise reserves of limestone and coal in the year 2004-05 are presented in Table 2. Garo Hills may have the largest reserves of coal, but mining is more intensive in Jaintia Hills (see Table 4). With the establishment of a few cement plants in Jaintia Hills, mining of limestone in Jaintia Hills has further intensified.

Table 2: Reserves of Major Minerals in Meghalaya in 2004-05

	Total Reserve in Million Tonnes	
Districts	*Coal*	*Limestone*
Khasi Hills	180	2,300
Jaintia Hills	40	1,100
Garo Hills	350	280
Total	**570**	**3,680**

Note: (a) Khasi Hills comprises East and West Khasi Hills
(b) Garo Hills includes East & West Garo Hills
Source: DMR, Government of Meghalaya

Official data in relation to production of all minerals (major and minor) are not available. The annual data in statistical books is arrived at on the basis of royalty collected and cess levied. It is known that unofficial trade is three to four times higher since trucks carry beyond the stipulated weight[5] implying that official data is grossly understated. Hence without regular assessments of estimated reserves and data of production, one would make wrong inferences.

According to the DMR, coal mining started in 1894 in the Khasi Hills and about 8,500 tonnes of coal were mined by the then Political Agent, and transported to Calcutta

5. See Dutta, 2000.

(Kolkata). Since the operations were uneconomical, future coal mining operations were left to the local miners to mine on a small-scale, cottage industry type, for their own domestic consumption. However, with the passage of time and with the opening up of road communication in these areas, the exploitation took place along commercial lines. The main market was Guwahati, Assam.

Table 3: Production of Major Minerals in Meghalaya in Selected Years (in '000 Metric Tonnes)

Year	*Coal*	*Limestone*
1970–71	61	87
1975–76	59	164
1980–81	521	234
1985–86	1,265	256
1990–91	2,241	205
1995–96	3,248	748
2005–06	5,629	1,044

Source: (i) *Statistical Handbook Meghalaya,* various issues, (ii) DMR, (iii) Department of Mining and Geology

Table 4: Production and Dispatch of Coal in the Period 1995-2005 (in '000 MT)

Year	*Jaintia Hills*	*Garo Hills*	*Khasi Hills*	*Total*
1995–96	2,159.5	889.2	188.8	3,247.5
1996–97	2,273.6	803.3	164.0	3,240.9
1997–98	2,414.6	599.4	119.5	3,233.5
1998–99	3,246.1	807.1	184.4	4,237.6
1999–2000	2,935.9	907.0	217.2	4,060.1
2000–01	2,839.9	1,017.7	207.3	4,064.9
2001–02	3,869.0	997.0	303.0	5,149.0
2002–03	3,084.4	910.7	401.1	4,396.2
2003–04	3,918.0	1,058.4	462.7	5,439.1
2004–05	3,610.6	1,101.0	633.4	5,345.0
2005–06	3,889.8	1,175.6	564.3	5,629.7
Grand Total	**34,241.4 (71. 3%)**	**10,266.4 (21. 4%)**	**3,445.7 (7. 2%)**	**48,043.5**

Note: Figures within ( ) are % of period total
Source: DMR, Government of Meghalaya

The productions of both coal and limestone increased significantly since attainment of statehood. Table 3 provides production data of selected years to illustrate this point. Limestone reserves are six times more than coal (Table 2) but, coal production has been more than double, except for the 1970s.

The mining and the volume of production is determined by accessibility and marketability. A district-wise break-up of the total production of coal for the period 1995-2006 is in Table 4.

In the given period, total production was 48,043.5 thousand MT with an annual average of 4,368 thousand MT. These figures are enormous given the crude and unscientific production methods involved. If the volume of unofficial trade is accounted for, the figures will inflate further. In the given period, the share of Jaintia Hills District of total production was the largest (71%), followed by Garo Hills (21%) and Khasi Hills (7%). The evident reasons for larger production in Jaintia Hills are relatively better road connectivity and exports via Dawki to Bangladesh. Official figures between 1994-2006 shows total exports to be 7,431

Table 5: Coal Exports to Bangladesh (in '000 MT)

Year	*Dawki*	*Borsora*	*Gasuapara*	*Total*
1994–95	191.354	33.258	49.265	273.877
1995–96	179.339	28.956	161.751	370.046
1996–97	283.298	40.144	115.229	438.671
1997–98	444.830	51.022	83.140	578.992
1998–99	498.678	60.151	36.895	595.724
1999–2000	293.055	79.063	70.662	442.780
2000–01	447.420	100.105	63.866	611.391
2001–02	474.722	203.826	76.484	755.032
2002–03	425.349	310.410	31.878	767.637
2003–04	480.695	365.922	28.960	875.577
2004–05	377.971	507.702	21.627	907.300
2005–06	396.841	398.981	18.192	814.014
Grand Total	**4,493.552**	**2,179.540**	**757.949**	**7,431.041**

Source: DMR, Government of Meghalaya

thousand MT. Total exports through Dawki in Jaintia Hills was 4,494 thousand MT or 60% of the total in the period. Borsora in West Khasi Hills and Gasuapara in Garo Hills are the other major land custom stations for exports to Bangladesh.

Table 6: Revenue Generation and Total Exporters

Particulars	*2003–04*	*2004–05*	*2005–06*
Check Gate	4	12	13
Revenue Collection (Rs.)	311,161,060	264,576,425	318,621,877
No. of Exporters	34	13	15
No. of Local Dealers	40	0	36

Source: DMR, 2007

Government Check Gates: (i) Byrnihat, (ii) Borsora, (iii) Daluagre, (iv) Dawki, (v) Dainadubi, (vi) Garampani, (vii) Gasuapara, (viii) Mookyndur, (ix) Mahendraganj, (x) Masangpani, (xi) Nidanpur, (xii) Riangdoh (Athiabari) and (xiii) Umkiang.

Table 7: Distribution of Enterprises Engaged in Mining and Quarrying by Type of Enterprises

District	*Total Number of Enterprises*											
	Rural				*Urban*				*Combined*			
	OAE	*NDE*	*DE*	*Total*	*OAE*	*NDE*	*DE*	*Total*	*OAE*	*NDE*	*DE*	*Total*
Jaintia Hills	116	60	94	270	0	1	17	18	116	61	111	288
East Khasi Hills	0	66	56	122	0	2	1	3	0	68	57	125
West Khasi Hills	0	0	1	1	0	1	0	1	0	1	1	2
East Garo Hills	0	0	0	0	6	1	0	7	6	1	0	7
West Garo Hills	21	2	1	24	0	0	0	0	21	2	1	24
Ri-Bhoi District	0	0	0	0	0	0	0	0	0	0	0	0
South Garo Hills	1	29	44	74	0	0	0	0	1	29	44	74
All Districts	138	157	196	491	6	5	18	29	144	162	214	520

Note: OAE – Own Account Enterprise, NDE – Non-Directory Enterprise, DE – Directory Enterprise

Source: *Report on Fourth Economic Census, 1998, Meghalaya Part 1 & II,* Directorate of Economics & Statistics

According to the *Fourth Economic Census of Meghalaya* in 1998, all mining and quarrying activities in the State were clubbed together. The actual number of coal mines and the ethnic background of workers remain unknown. Information relating to enterprises in mining and quarrying for the entire State is in Table 7.

What the above table only reveals are the number of enterprises engaged in mining and quarrying in different districts and their nature. It is not possible to determine how many are mining and/or quarrying what. Apart from limestone and coal, the above figures also include mining and quarrying of rock aggregates of sand and clays and mining/quarrying of minerals for construction other than those just mentioned. An Own Account Enterprise (OAE) is owned and operated with the help of household members only, and by this definition, we can logically omit all enterprises under this category as not being involved in coal and limestone mining. Non-Directory Enterprise (NDE) and Directory Enterprise (DE) are treated as establishments because at least more than one worker is hired on a regular basis. While NDEs are enterprises with 1 to 5 hired workers, DEs are enterprises with more than 5 hired workers. Moreover, with mining sites usually located in rural areas, coal and mining activities will be recorded under the categories of NDEs and DEs in the rural areas. Hence, coal and limestone mining activities will fall under these categories. As per the same report, the district-wise concentration of mining and quarrying (enterprises per thousand population) was the highest in Jaintia Hills with a share of 1.03 against 0.24 for Meghalaya. Of the total 520 enterprises, only one was government-owned and 136 enterprises had completed more than 9 years of operation. 502 were 'self-financing', 3 borrowed from 'institutions' and 15 from 'non-institutions and others', and none of the 520 enterprises were registered with any agency.

4.1 Distribution of Limestone

Limestone is found to occur in abundance in the State of Meghalaya, particularly in the southern border extending for about 200 kms. from Jaintia Hills in the east to Garo Hills in the west. Practically all the three hills, namely Khasi, Jaintia and Garo Hills contain limestone of variable quantity and quality. The quality of the limestone found here varies from cement grade to chemical grade. There are some limestones in Meghalaya that are suitable for manufacture of Precipitated Calcium Carbonate (PCC). The quality of limestone in the State has CaO content of 53% and can be of great use to the steel, fertiliser and chemical industries.

1. Khasi Hills

(a) Cherrapunji: This deposit is located in the Mawmluh-Mawsmai Hills south of lower Cherra. The deposit is about 1.40 kms. in area. The deposit is of a composite nature, made up of limestone in the upper part and dolomite in the lower part. A reserve of limestone and dolomite from this deposit as reported by GSI was 40 million tonnes. At present the Mawmluh Cherra Cement factory exists in the area.

(b) Laitryngew: The deposit occurs near Umstrew and Mawkma areas of Laitryngew.

(c) Mawlong-Ishamati: The extent of the deposit is about 13.75 sq. kms. with a reserve of 2,166 million tonnes. The limestone is hard and compact, grey dark-grey to bluish grey in colour, fine-grained and fossiliferous.

(d) Komorrah: This is located near Komorrah (near Shella) in the east Khasi Hills that is about 0.52 sq. kms. with a reserve of 14.2 million tonnes. Limestone occurs in alternate bands of sandstone. The limestone is hard, compact, fine-grained and fossiliferous.

(e) Shella: The deposit is located on the west bank of the Umiew river near Shella Bazar covering an area of 2.76 sq. kms. The limestone is hard, compact, light grey to dark grey in colour with an estimated reserve of 180 million tones.

(f) Borsora: The area lies to the north of the Indo-Bangladesh border of West Khasi Hills. The area is about 1 sq. km. with reserves of about 37 million tonnes. The limestone is light grey in colour, jointed and highly fractured.

2. *Jaintia Hills*

Lumshnong-Mynkre: Highgrade limestone is found to occur near Lumshnong covering an area of 76.8 sq. kms. with an estimated reserve of 652 million tonnes. The CMCL (Cement Manufacturing Company Limited) has been producing 'Star Cement' from the limestones of this area. The extraction of limestone from the area has put the cave system in the area under threat. The Meghalaya Adventure Association in 2006 filed a PIL with the hope that the longest cave system in Asia is saved. Other reserves are Nongkhlieh (south of Khliehriat on Jowai-Badarpur Road), Lakadong and Syndai (Jowai-Muktapur Road).

3. *Garo Hills*

The major limestone area in Garo Hills is the Siju-Artheka area which is situated at 118 kms. from Dudhnai along Dudhnai-Baghmara Road in the southeast of Garo Hills. Limestone occurs on both sides of river Simsang. The limestone is hard and greenish grey in colour. Other deposits occur at Darrang-Era-Aning near Nangabibra.

4.2 Limestone Development

Limestone mining in the State, unlike coal, is more or less in the organised sector. It is therefore only in limestone mining that we find outside companies investing here in the State. Though limestone reserve is far greater than coal, yet the extraction and production of coal is far greater than that of limestone. Coal mine owners say that this is so because coal fetched more revenue than limestone. What we see in limestone is that the mineral is taken mostly to cement factories outside the State. The various companies that have invested and mined in the State are:

1. Lafarge Umiam Mining Pvt. Ltd. (LUMPL) at Shella, Nongtrai of East Khasi Hills District. Here, the company exports limestone to Lafarge Surma Cement in Bangladesh. Recently the Supreme Court asked the company to stop work on the basis of the petition filed by the Ministry of Environment and Forests on the plea that the 17 km-long conveyor belt passes through a forested area. This was contrary to the permission granted based on the Environment Impact Assessment obtained from Delhi-based Environment Resource Management Pvt. Ltd. stating that the 100 acre area of the belt and the mining area are waste land. This is clearly a violation of the norms and the environmental laws governing it. The Supreme Court, in an interim order on November 23, 2007 allowed Lafarge to continue mining limestone. The Shella Action Committee (SAC) asked International Foreign Corporation (IFC) to stop funding to LUMPL as it was opposed to the secret 'mortgage of land' belonging to the indigenous people to foreign banks. The SAC planned to challenge the court order.[6] The Supreme Court on July 6, 2011 directed LUMPL to pay a certain amount to the State Government for compensatory afforestation from 2007 towards Compensatory Afforestation Fund Management and Planning Authority (CAMPA).
2. Cement Manufacturing Company Ltd. (CMCL) started captive mining of limestone at Lumshnong in Jaintia Hills. It also depends on local suppliers for the supply of coal, limestone and other materials. It produces 'Star Cement'. This again has faced stiff resistance from the people over the threat of

6. *The Shillong Times*, May 9, 2008.

destroying the various cave systems in the area owing to the use of explosives. The Meghalaya Adventure Association (MAA) filed a PIL describing the damaged done to the 21 km. Kotsati-Umlawan cave system which is said to be the longest cave system in the country.

3. Mawmluh Cherra Cement Ltd. is a state-owned undertaking with production capacity of 930 tpd located at Mawmluh and Cherra of Khasi Hills. It is currently able to meet the domestic demand.
4. Komorrah Limestone Mining Ltd., Shella, is a joint venture enterprise with the Government of Meghalaya operating limestone mining for export to Chhatak Cement in Bangladesh.
5. Meghalaya Minerals and Mines Pvt. Ltd. operating at Lumshnong, Jaintia Hills, mines limestone and export it to Barak Valley Cements Ltd. in Assam.
6. Meghalaya Cements Ltd. at Thangskai (Jaintia Hills) produces the well-known 'Topcem Cement'. The Lumshnong Students Association raised concerns of pollution in streams and rivers due to the discharge from the factories. The company has assured, though, to launch a separate water supply scheme for the villagers.
7. K. Singh Wann and Sons at Ishamati in Khasi Hills.

In 2013, there were nine cement companies operating in the State, mostly in Jaintia Hills District. These were Adhunik Cement, Amrit Cement Industries, Cement Manufacturing Company, Cosmos Cement, Green Valley Industries, Goldstone Cement, Hills Cement, JUD Cements and Meghalaya Cement. More cement companies are waiting for the government's clearance for their operation. Dalmia (Bharat) Ltd. entered northeast in general and Meghalaya in particular by acquiring two cement manufacturing units in the region, i.e. Calcom Cement Ltd and Adhunik Cement in Thangskai, East Jaintia Hills. The approximate cement produced from the State is more than 5 million metric tonnes per annum.

The Joint Inspection Team (JIT) formed in 2011 found that nearly 50% of the total surveyed land under the nine cement plants in the Jaintia Hills district was classified as forest and found to have violated provisions of the Forest Conservation Act, 1980. These companies have now agreed to buy double the land misused by them and subsequently use them as part of afforestation programmes. The Meghalaya Transfer of Land (Regulation), 1971 does not allow the cement plants to purchase land in the State. It is for this reason that the government is preparing modalities through which government will acquire land on behalf of cement plants. This would, however, complicate matters as forest, land and water are depleting and are in a deplorable condition in the mining areas.

4.3 Distribution of Coal

Coal deposits can be found in the districts of Garo Hills, West Khasi Hills and Jaintia Hills. This coal bears low ash content and its calorific value ranges from 6,500 to 7,500 kcal/kg. The coal is mainly of sub-bituminous type and can be used in varied industries ranging from power, fertiliser, cement and textile to paper, rubber, brick burning and pottery-based industries. The coal that is found in the State can also be converted into coke and recover value-added chemicals like light, medium and heavy oil, phenol, xynelol and producer gas. The tertiary coal deposits of Meghalaya, belonging to the Eocene age, are found to be mostly on the southern slopes of the State. The main characteristics of the coal obtained here are its low ash content, high volatile matter and also high calorific value. However, it has a drawback of high sulphur content. Owing to the inconsistent nature of the coal seams coupled with complicated geological structures in certain areas, it is rather difficult to ascertain the actual reserves of the deposits. The inferred reserves of the major deposits, as estimated periodically, are indicated below under the description of each deposit.

1. Khasi Hills

(a) Mawsynram: Coal in Mawsynram area occurs at Rangsokham, Jathan, Lumbidon and Mosing. Coal is generally soft powdery, but it is hard and lumpy where it attains maximum thickness, with an estimated reserve of 0.32 million tonnes.

(b) Lumdidom: Situated near Mawsynram, it has an area of 0.2 sq. kms. The coal is bright, compact and shally. The indicated reserve in the Lumdidom area is 0.2 million tonnes.

(c) Langrin: The Langrin Coalfield is situated in the south-western extremity of the West Khasi Hills extending to Borsora. There are seven coal seams with an estimated reserve of 97.61 million tonnes. This is a major coal mining and exporting area after Garo Hills and Jaintia Hills.

(d) Other fields in the Khasi Hills are Laitryngew, Laitduh, Laitryngew, Mahbelakar, Mawsynram (East Khasi Hills), Wah Rangah, Nangmawli and Nongmaharu (West Khasi Hills).

2. Garo Hills

(a) East Darrangiri: This area lies in the border of Khasi Hills and Garo Hills district covering an area of 21 sq. kms. The reserve here as reported by GSI is 31.50 million tonnes.

(b) West Darrangiri: This is the most accessible and most exploitable coal deposit in the State with an area of 25 sq. kms. and reserve of 127 million tonnes, the largest in the State. Coal India Limited started exploration in the area for a while, but since then they have not started mining. The other coal fields in the district are Asilgaon Hill, Ronrenggiri (Simsang River), Siju, Pendengru-balpakram and Selsella coalfields.

3. *Jaintia Hills*

(a) Bapung: Bapung is situated at a distance of 24 kms. from Jowai Town along Jowai-Badarpur Road, occupying an area of 46 sq. kms. with the probable reserve of 33.66 million tonnes. The coal is good having low ash and moisture content, but the sulphur is high.

(b) Jarain and Tkentalang: This is from Jarain to Mawpang. The coal is bright and hard lump coal, but the coal of the Jarain area is soft and friable. The area is 2.8 sq. kms. and reserve of 1.1 million tonnes.

(c) Other coalfields are Lakadong, where the two important fields are Pamsaru and Umlatdoh (reserve 4,70,000 tonnes), Khliehriat, Lad Rymbai, Musiang Lamare (near Lumshnong) and Sutnga.

4.4 Uranium

Domiasiat, a small hamlet in West Khasi Hills District of the State of Meghalaya, is about 130 kms. from Shillong, the State capital. This 'little once unknown place' recently came into the limelight and could be the much talked about place in the country. Domiasiat is, more or less, an untouched world since there is no connectivity with the outside world. A curious explorer would have to trek through a rugged topography for an hour and a half to reach there. What is even more challenging is riding on rooftops of a bi-weekly bus through an unsurfaced road to reach Wahkaji, which is the closest village.

This hamlet sits on the Khasi Series of granite belonging to the cretaceous period. There is also an abundance of red and yellow sandstones accompanied by old alluvium. The rainfall is as heaviest as any southern slope of Meghalaya. Few have equated it to that of Cherrapunji. The soil is rich and fertile housing a variety of vegetations. It is also one of the richest biosphere reserves in the State. Several indigenous tree species and fruit trees can be seen growing on the slopes of the hills. A carnivorous plant species called the Pitcher

Plant (locally known as *Tongsnoi*) is found in abundance. During the summer, one can enjoy the lush green meadows and the several rivulets making it quite poetic and nostalgic. But one has to bear the endurance of the blood-sucking leeches that can cling to the body in an instant when passing through. Locals carry along with them a mixture of lime, tobacco and salt to avoid any clinging of these tiny but creepy creatures.

This hamlet is about 15 sq. kms. in area having only about eight families residing in it, all belonging to one ruling clan called the *Langrin*. The land is often leased out to people for a period of one to two years at a very reasonable rate. The people use the land for shifting cultivation. They cultivate the slopes by clearing the forest. Wood is converted to charcoal, which remains the primary occupation, besides broomsticks. They also grow crops like rice, maize, millets, pepper, areca nut and fruits and vegetables for their own sustenance.About 23 villages surround Domiasiat in all directions. These villages are within a radius of 5-10 kms. The total population would be about 5,000. The region is backward with no proper facilities like drinking water, sanitation and electricity. The transport and communication network has yet to be developed here. The Christian missionaries have established churches and educational institutions that have made the people more rational in outlook.

In the year 1991-92, the Department of Atomic Power, Government of India, found a trace of rich uranium in the periphery. It was estimated to be one of the best in terms of quality and is also at a more shallow depth of 10-50 feet from the crust. It was said that this was a new find after the four-decade-old mining at Jadugoda in Jharkhand is almost depleted. The Uranium Corporation of India Limited (UCIL) started exploration on an experimental basis at the site called Nongbah Jynrin, which is 5 kms. south of Domiasiat. The estimated reserve of uranium according to UCIL is to the tune of 10,000 tonnes. The Domiasiat deposit is, according to

UCIL, the largest, richest, near surface and low-cost, sandstone-type uranium deposit discovered in India so far. The ores are spread over a 10 sq. kms. area (6 sq. miles) in deposits varying from eight to 47 metres from the surface.

According to S Syiem, the headman of Domiasiat, the Atomic Mineral Department (AMD) started exploratory work in 1983 when permission for testing was granted. In 1989 the villagers found out that a large number of people, mostly labourers from outside the State, had camped at the site. They had already extracted the ore and transported it outside the area. When the headman came to know of this, he met the AMD officials and asked for an explanation as to why extraction of the mineral took place when permission was granted only for survey and not extraction. The people from Domiasiat protested against this and the local MLA H S Lyngdoh vehemently opposed the whole operation. In 1991 the AMD officials left the place. The sealed pits can be seen at two places at Domiasiat.

Due to the fear of severe repercussions resulting from radiation and repetition of the health hazards that ravage Jadugoda, several non-governmental organisations and the public at large protested and resisted the extraction of uranium. This made the UCIL to cease work and abandoned the place. Now there is only the remnant of dugout pits, which are meticulously, covered by thick concrete.

UCIL recently tried to go around the Khasi Autonomous District Hills Council (KHADC) by submitting a proposal to the state government to mine the uranium at Domiasiat. The proposal contains an economic development package and a proposal to create a helipad for the air transportation of uranium ore from Domiasiat to UCIL headquarters at Jadugoda in Jharkhand. Under the economic development package, the Corporation vows to construct roads and bridges in the area, and provide employment for about 800 local people. This is at an estimated cost of Rs. 450 crores. About 30,000 people are likely to be displaced by full-scale mining, although UCIL is promising to provide 85% of the jobs to residents in the area. 'The UCIL is soon to start mining operations at Domiasiat in the West Khasi Hills of Meghalaya', reports *The Northeast Daily*. It stated that under the Atomic Energy Act, the central government has all rights to assume authority of the area and will initiate mining operations, despite stiff opposition from the local people and the Khasi Hills Autonomous District Council (KHADC).

According to UCIL sources, 'an agreement has been concluded into between the UCIL and the landowners for transfer of land for the proposed project on annual lease of Rs. 15,000 per hectare with an increase of 5% every year'. Further, it went on to say, that the government and the KHADC will be paid Rs. 60 lakhs as royalty per annum. About Rs. 25 lakhs have been earmarked for socio-economic development of the area.[7] The former KHADC executive member and former mining and geology minister, P K Raswai, said that the KHADC has not issued a 'no-objection certificate' to date, which the UCIL needs to proceed with mining. However, he agreed that it is possible for the central government to come forward directly to mine uranium or any other minerals in the state.

What the people are looking for at the moment is a clarification from the various groups and organisations about the much talked about uranium mining. Out of the earmarked money of Rs. 450 crores for the project at Domiasiat, some would go for development purposes like construction of proper roads, establishment of hospitals, dispensaries, schools, post offices and many others. This would certainly benefit the people of the region. But uncertainty looms over for they are apprehensive that they might be alienated from their lands, lose their property and even fear that these promises might not actually be for them but to the employees of the corporation only. The crucial question that hovers all over the region is whether their health will be at stake at the cost of development.

7. *The Shillong Times*, May 2007.

Recently a newspaper reported that uranium had been exploited and transported from Tiniang village near Domiasiat to the AMD office at Shillong for the last three to four years. It was on this truth that reports of 'strange illnesses' have been reported from Phlangdiloin, Pyndemsynnia by the Langrin Youth Welfare Association with evidential photographs.[8] Based on the report, a medical team visited Phangdilion village on December 13, 2005 and organised a health camp on the day. At least 376 people, including 169 males and 207 females, in the age group of 0 to 80 years had checkups in the health camp so as to enable the officials to have a conclusive report on the health hazards that uranium mining could have caused. The non-governmental organisations (NGOs) recently claimed that the waste piles left from exploration for uranium a few years ago had affected the general health of the people. The team said that contrary to the claim of NGOs, there was no apparent effect of radiation on the general health of the people residing around the mining areas. 'There was only one case of radio oncology strongly suggesting an advance carcinoma of the throat case, besides a few skin problems like scabies and seborrhea dermatitis. There was no endemic of any particular disease, but the people suffered from common ailments', the report said adding that infection of the upper and lower respiratory tract and acid peptic diseases were prevalent, while essential hypertension, diabetes mellitus and chronic amoebiasis were not detected. The report, however, observed that the medical team could not cover Domiasiat village on the same day as 'the area was not easily accessible'.[9]

The Atomic Energy Commission (AEC) has decided to change the name of the proposed uranium mining project in West Khasi Hills to Kylleng-Pyndemsohiong-Mawthabah Uranium Mining Project, instead of Domiasiat Uranium

8. Photographs on *Maitshaphrang* Magazine, Vol. 1, No. 3 July-November 2005.
9. *The Shillong Times*, December 21, 2005.

Mining Project. According to their opinion, the name of the project had been changed after proper verification by the Atomic Minerals Division (AMD) and State Government which revealed that there was 'no uranium deposit at the site of the present Domiasiat uranium mining project'.[10] Yet UCIL is keen to start uranium mining at Domiasiat and stated that all precautionary measures have been taken. Accordingly, 'various pre-project activities like preparation of the Environment Impact Assessment (EIA)/Environment Management Plan (EMP) Report, Detailed Project Report (DPR) have been initiated' by them, which seems to be contrary to what (UCIL) Chairman-cum-Managing (CMD) Director R Gupta reiterated: 'We will start the project only after we convince the people that the project is in their interest, the project will only be started with public approval.'

4.5 The Debate

A debate amongst representatives from various groups was held on July 15, 2004 at Shillong. The UCIL, BARC, DAE, and AMD Shillong, well-known journalists, physicists, and activists from Jadugoda (Jharkhand), Shillong and West Khasi Hills were prominent in the discussion besides a sizeable number of the audience. The speakers in the debate, amongst others included, P Bidwai, reputed columnist, who dealt with the genetic problems of toxicity of uranium, occupational hazards and environmental consequences. Dr Gadekar, a Physicist, Professor IIT, Kanpur presented on development and health. Dr R Gupta, CMD of UCIL reiterated that mining will bring development in the area and the region as a whole. S K Malhotra from the Department of Atomic Energy, while elaborating on the risks of the fuel cycle, said 'risks are there even in aeroplanes and even in railways. Risks are everywhere'. Gyansham from Jharkhand highlighted UCIL's false promises of giving jobs to local

---

10. *The Shillong Times*, March 14, 2005.

people which did not materialise even after 40 years. Instead, mysterious diseases have emerged in the area with people suffering from impotency, stillborn babies, birth of children without limbs, etc. which were unheard of in the past.

The three organisations, viz. Khasi Students Union (KSU), Meghalaya People's Human Right Council (MPHRC), and Hynniewtrep Environment Status Preservation Organisation (HESPO) resolved that they are not in favour of uranium mining due to (a) health hazards, (b) land displacement and (c) influx of foreigners. They concluded by saying that 'we, the three organisations, don't want development at the cost of the generation at stake'. Thus, the resolution declared: 'We stand against the uranium mining in Meghalaya and resolved to pressurise the government to abolish the uranium agenda.'

Some sources say that the growing nuclear arms race in South Asia has created pressure for the Domiasat yellowcake reserves to be exploited. Officials from UCIL and BARC, which is connected with nuclear weapons programmes in India, have visited Domiasiat several times in recent years. The Australian and US governments are also keen to start a joint venture with the Government of India on nuclear plants.

UCIL's Domiasiat proposal received a boost when the high-level team, which visited Jaduguda in Jharkhand to gather firsthand knowledge on uranium mining, virtually gave its seal of approval allaying fear of ill effects. The KHADC Chief Executive Member P Tynsong said the team did not witness ill-effects of mining on human life, vegetations, and animals there.[11] But then the KHADC decided to first, seek a White Paper from the UCIL on the advantages and disadvantages of uranium mining at Domiasiat in West Khasi Hills district. The decision to this effect was taken at a meeting held in Shillong on March 7, 2005 between the KHADC officials and traditional heads of Nongstoin and Langrin.[12]

11. *The Shillong Times*, July 14, 2005.
12. *The Shillong Times*, March 8, 2005.

4.6 Anti-mining Lobby

Those who vehemently oppose the project of uranium at Domiasiat and the surrounding area are the three organisations spearheading the movement, i.e. the KSU, MPHRC and HESPO. H S Lyngdoh, the political leader from the region, has been able to be firm in his stand since the time uranium mining was at the exploratory stages. He has been to world forums to get more information on the effects of mining, and several times he was even denied a visa to attend such meetings and conferences. Others who are at the forefront opposing such a move by the KHADC and the government are John F Kharshiing who is the chairman of Ka Dorbar Ki Nongsynshar Ka Ri Hynniewtrep which is an Assembly of Hynniewtrep Traditional Rulers, noted author and social activist Arundhati Roy, B Lyngdoh, a member of the World Commission of Young Leaders for the United Nations and some organisations like Western Youth Welfare Organisation (WYWO), NADO, NAIDO, and Lai Lyngdoh Welfare Organisation (LYWO). A few of them come under the umbrella of the newly-formed Coordination Committee against Uranium Mining (CCAUM).

4.7 Pro-mining

On the other side there are not many who would openly welcome the mining project. The UCIL has support from the KHADC and the government. The two play their cards carefully since intricacies involved are too delicate. Recently the KHADC Chief Executive Member, H S Shylla, while addressing another debate at Shillong, said 'do not speak of health hazards until you are ready to file a review petition on the Supreme Court ruling'.[13] The only people's organisation seeking early operation of the project is the Langrin War-San Lyngdoh Development Organisation or LWLDO. Several rallies were held near Domiasiat which was

13. *NEHU News*, Vol. 7, No. 2, April-June 2006.

attended by people of several villages. The rally welcomed the proposed uranium project while also urging the State Government to grant permission to UCIL to start the mining process.

4.8 Steps Taken by the State Government

A high-level committee headed by the then Chief Minister of Meghalaya Dr D D Lapang has been constituted to examine all issues related to the proposed uranium mining project at Domiasiat. The Cabinet Committee on Economic Affairs (CCEA) will be the nodal department for such an initiative. The committee will examine all issues related to the project, including health issues, and will make recommendations to the Cabinet for its approval.

4.9 Project Take Off or Standstill

The UCIL has already financed a road project through the KHADC which would be constructed at an estimated cost of Rs.100 million. Rs.9.6 million was released by UCIL to KHADC for the road project. The proposed 20 km. road would connect Wahkaji with seven villages including Mawthabah. Work orders were given without tender notices and this irked several people who felt that UCIL had made false promises. The proposed laying of the foundation stone of the new road from Wahkaji to Mawthabah by the Atomic Energy Commission Chairman Dr Anil Kakodkar was opposed and did not materialise. A portion of the already constructed road was destroyed in the agitation following the blockade.

4.10 The Public Hearing

The Ministry of Forests and Environment, Government of India, instructed the State Government to initiate a Public Hearing as mandatory before mining actually starts. Few opined that this might be too early as the issue was not clear to the people. After days of debates, discussions and opposition, the government decided to go ahead with the proposed hearing. The Public Hearing was conducted by the Meghalaya State Pollution Control Board (MPCB) at Nongbah Jynrin, West Khasi Hills on June 12, 2007. In a dramatic turn of events, a large majority of the people from the area opposed the proposed uranium mining on the ground of health hazards, while those who supported the project constituted only 25%. The villagers from adjoining areas of Nongbah Jynrin like Umdohlun, Wahkaji and Phlangdiloin were vociferous in their opposition.

4.11 Recent Developments

The Department of Atomic Energy, Government of India, signed a memorandum with the State Government to open a Cancer Unit at the Shillong Civil Hospital at the cost of Rs. 25 crores. The visit by the then Union Minister of State for Power, Jairam Ramesh, had created ripples as he categorically stated that a nuclear plant will be set up in the northeast and preferably in Meghalaya. He went on to say that 'most of our nuclear power plants are running at 50% capacity due to shortage of uranium. This shortage is the reason why we are opting for the Indo-US nuclear deal. Uranium from Meghalaya can help us feed our nuclear reactors to a great extent'. A white paper will be presented which will mention the DAE's plan for uranium mining in Meghalaya and the precautions it would take to address the fears of the locals. Meanwhile Deputy Chief Minister, Hopping Stone Lyngdoh, who spearheaded the anti-mining lobby and now in the government said that 'we have no such plans and will oppose any move to set up a nuclear power plant or mine uranium in the state'. The Union Minister later, feeling the pulse of the present government, admitted that 'the central government will not do anything against the wishes of the Government of Meghalaya or the public opinion of the state. This is a huge challenge and we will address it in a very transparent manner'.

4.12 Mining Policy on the Anvil

The issue of mining in the State received some serious attention as the draft State Mining Policy is reported to be ready for adoption after being in the public domain for suggestions for a long time. There are many grey areas which need to be sorted like clarity on mining 'within or outside forest areas' being foremost. Further, consensus on every section of the policy is most unlikely since absolute authority and freedom enjoyed by individual miners and mine owners on nature and mode of mining shall be curbed together with provision for protection of the eco-system. Scientific mining and environment protection measures including mine safety infrastructure entail additional expenditure, which most miners will resist. However, the delay in adoption may be a blessing in disguise for the common man residing in mining areas. A bill that promises direct benefit to people from the minerals underneath their land was ready to be tabled in Parliament which requires mining companies to shell out a portion of their profit for people displaced or affected by their operations. The bill will replace the existing Mines and Minerals Development and Regulation (MMDR) Act of 1957. The profit-sharing provision in the MMDR Bill of 2011 requires mining including coal companies to share their net profit—26%, every year with the affected communities. Companies that mine major minerals like limestone and iron ore will have to give the affected people an amount equal to the royalty that they pay to the state government annually. For those mining minor minerals like sandstone and marble, the states will decide the profit-sharing percentage in consultation with the proposed National Mining Regulatory Authority. It is essential for mining companies to pay 26% of their annual profit or 100% of the royalty, whichever is higher, to communities. This would not apply to the nationalised coal sector, which would pay 26% of the profit. In Meghalaya the situation is complex and the mining policy can only address the issue to factor in the salient features of the MMDR Bill. The same may not be applicable to coal mines particularly, which escaped nationalisation and individual mine owners have absolute rights over the coal extracted from their individual mines including pricing except for paying a small royalty to the government. This is the first time the concept of natural resource rent is being established in the country. In this age of green accounting, the wealth of the nation is valued in terms of its value to equity and sustainability. Green growth is fundamentally about inclusive growth. The Meghalaya Mining Policy can factor in the essence of the bill and make it mandatory for coal miners, and in the case of other minerals like limestone, the manufacturer/company utilising the minerals as raw materials to produce an end product to pay a fixed amount to the community inhabiting the mining areas. This will ensure sustainable development of the people and environment both of which are suffering due to mining, including those displaced or affected by such operations. The approach of the policy has to be sustainable development of people and not sustainable development of mining. The fund so generated can be used, for example, in amelioration of ground water and treating highly contaminated water run-off from mines due to high sulphur content in coal mining areas of Jaintia Hills. Treatment of abandoned mines and the adverse effect on agricultural land is another sector which requires immediate attention to avoid a looming environment catastrophe. Apart from greenhouse gas emissions, the fact of the matter is that, in India, mining has led to large-scale degradation of the environment. Mining cannot be stopped or wished away however hard one tries. Then there are various economic considerations and utilisation of minerals for production of end product like cement, for example.The best out of a worst situation is to strike a realistic balance between industrial growths, mining and accrual of maximum possible benefit to the State and its people with priority on protection of environment.

5

The Current Situation: A Case Study of Coal Mining in Jaintia Hills

This study was undertaken to record the ground realities of coal mining. The foremost problem encountered was the difficulty to get primary data due to the reluctance to share accurate information. It is thus a narrative based on interviews and observations made in the mining and other sites of prevalent mining practices, the procedures involved, the type of workers engaged at different stages, the conditions they worked and lived in and finally, the consequences of such activities on the ecology.

Due to the land holding pattern in Meghalaya, licenses and MOUs are not mandatory for any form of mining activity, unless it is an industrial unit. Hence, virtually all coal-mining activities fall in the unorganised sector. Individuals mining coal have been accorded the status of cottage type industries and are recognised as such by both state and central governments. In short, these ventures do not come under the preview of any mining law as applicable in other parts of the country.

The erratic and narrow seams of coal prevent scientific mining and the use of sophisticated tools and machinery is economically unviable. Therefore, extensive usage is made of rudimentary tools such as spades and pickaxes. Over the decades, countless mines have been carved and dug spreading randomly across the length and breadth of the coal bearing areas. The findings after visiting Ladrymbai, Longkaluh, Sutnga, Myrsiang, Nongjri, Waliang, Narwan, Jalaphet Sumer, Jarain, Mukhain and Mookympad are discussed under the following headings:

(a) Particulars of Coal Mining in surveyed areas
(b) Economic and social consequences of mining
(c) Areas of concern: Health and Environment

a. Particulars of Coal Mining in Surveyed Areas

Among the major minerals of Meghalaya, the most intensively mined is coal. Of the total 570 million tonnes estimated reserves of coal, the least (40 thousand MT or 7%) is located in the Jaintia Hills District where it is most extensively extracted, accounting for 71% of total production (Table 4). Coal mining started in Jaintia Hills in 1974 with an annual production of 5.4 thousand tonnes and by 2006 it had increased by more than 1,042 times.

The high calorific value of the coal from Jaintia Hills makes it useful in brick manufacturing industries. Underground mining and surface or 'rat–hole' mining are the two operational methods depending upon the depth of the coal beds. In the first method, coal is extracted from the side of the hills. In the second method, deeper beds of coal are extracted. Owing to the almost complete exhaustion of surface coal, underground mining is becoming the prevalent practice. The first step is to vertically dig a large rectangle to a depth of 90 to 140 feet. The depth depends on the coal seams as well as on the availability of finances. 'A large rectangle of at least 90 feet depth takes almost two years to complete at a cost of almost Rs. 10 lakhs', said a mine manager. The site to excavate is based entirely on luck. No scientific inputs are used. A proposed site is determined by drawing imaginary lines from a distant neighbour's coal pit. Deserted pits tell the story of several unsuccessful endeavours. However, when one does find coal seams, and the assumed safety norm is reached, the digging meanders and follows the small erratic seams. Some of these tunnels or 'rat–holes' have made their way under residential areas and roads. People narrated the caving in of houses and roads. One particular story is shared by a few inhabitants about the cruelty of mine owners and the politics that they play: 'An excavation was underway and miners wanted to pass through an area where a church was situated. The priest resisted. The mine owner brought in the police. They led the priest just past a hill and shot him dead because he was meddling in the miners' affairs.'

In respect of ownership of mines, the local inhabitants (Pnars) were found to have a greater share than the Khasis. Starting a new coal pit is risky and an expensive venture and we can presume partnerships/joint-ventures between indigenous people and non-locals. There is also the possibility of leasing based on verbal agreements and therefore unknown to others. Since owners are rarely in the mining sites only a few 'Sordars'/Managers were willing to answer our queries

Different sets of workers were engaged in different stages of mining from digging to unloading of coal in depots along the roadside with an overwhelming number were non-locals. The 'Sordars' or Managers were either Nepalis or Bengalis. At the bottom of the pits were the diggers using pickaxes. They were Nepali and Bihari. They had to crawl into the tunnels using torchlights, dig and then extract the coal (using small wooden carts) to another wooden box (measuring 6 x 4 x 4 feet) at the bottom of the pit. A full box earned them Rs.700. The rates varied on the basis of mine depth and tunnel length. The pace of work at this stage was exceptionally strenuous and slow.

The next step was to carry the coal from the box at the bottom of the pit to other boxes of similar dimensions at the top. The workers performing this task were Nepali, Bihari and in some mines Nagas and Kukis and, in a few isolated cases, Pnars. Using indigenously made baskets or *Khohs* slung over their backs, these workers carried about 30 kgs. on every ascent treading slowly over treacherous looking makeshift ladders to the top. Here too, the rates varied between Rs. 140 to Rs. 160 per basket depending on the depth of mines. On an average, 30 baskets filled a box measuring 6 x 4 x 4 feet. The average per day was 1 or 2 boxes.

The coal from these boxes was then loaded into four-wheeled vehicles like *Shaktimans* by another group of workers. Nepali and Bihari workers usually loaded the trucks. Nagas, Kukis and local Pnars in some cases, were reported and observed. The laden trucks transported and unloaded the coal in wide open spaces or roadside depots. Hired daily wage earners were used to first unload and then load the coal into trucks bound for different destinations like Silchar in Assam, Beltola in Guwahati, Assam and to Bangladesh via Dawki (around 10% of total production of Jaintia Hills District). As mentioned earlier, of the total coal exports from Meghalaya, 60% is from Jaintia Hills via Dawki (Table 8). The current export rate for coal is $ 40 per tonne and royalty collection by the State Government is Rs. 165 per tonne.

The regular workers in the coal mines resided in temporary dwellings at the site. Almost 99% of the workforce was males and non-tribals. There were a few female workers (adults and children) working in the depots. Females also worked at the initial stages of mining, usually cleaning the debris. The study found the youngest worker to be 17 years and the eldest 49 years. The middle-aged helped in repair of tools and in stockpiling of coal at the sites. It is only in the recent past that local tribals have taken up work in coal mines in different capacities in Sutnga area.

b) Economic and Social Consequences of Mining

According to the Population Census 2001, Jaintia Hills District had a population of 2 99,108 of which, 92% were rural-based. Total workers (main and marginal) comprised 42% of the total population. 47% the total workers were 'cultivators', 29% were 'agricultural labourers', 2% were involved in the 'household sector', and the remaining 22%

comprised 'other workers'. This last category includes labourers involved in mining and quarrying (coal, limestone and those involved in mining other minor minerals). 'Other workers' also include government servants, municipal employees, teachers, factory workers, plantation workers, those engaged in trade, commerce, business, transport, banking, construction, political or social work, priests, entertainment artists, etc. The primary survey allows us to infer that a very small percent of the local people are workers at any stage of mining of coal. Consequently, the economic benefits are negligible. Apart from the mine owners from the coal bearing areas, most people in the Jaintia Hills District are involved in agriculture. Secondary data of Khliehriat sub-division where the major coal reserves are located and mined, leads to similar conclusions.

Khliehriat, as per the Population Census 2001, had 15,517 households with a population of 92,792 (or 31% of the entire district's population). The average household size was 6 and the Scheduled Tribe population was 95%. The literacy level was 48%. Out of the total population, 51% were main and marginal workers with worker participation rate of 44.3, with higher participation rate for males at 49.2 than females at 39.3. Of the total working population, 50% were 'cultivators', 28% 'agricultural labourers', 4% were engaged in 'household industries' and the remaining 18% were grouped as 'other workers'. The chief occupation continues to remain agriculture which is either for subsistence or semi-commercial.

Though coal mining is labour-intensive offering higher monetary returns, the local people have stayed away. Some say that the hazard of mining keeps them at bay. Others observe that it is cheaper to employ migrant labourers. As a result, a large number of workers from others parts of India and countries like Bangladesh and Nepal have thronged these areas to make up for the labour scarcity. This has affected the demographic profile of the region which is not entirely evident since most workers stay in their respective sites.

Moreover, since the Mines Act is not applicable, the workers are not registered. The daily wage earners reside in groups in small towns that have mushroomed along the national highway. In these places, small businesses are controlled by non-tribals (over 90%) selling items like shoes, cloths, food items, spare parts for automobiles, wine, etc. The state government has proposed to implement identity cards for migrant labourers based on the ongoing protests and actions of local pressure groups.

Basic infrastructure was virtually absent. Many villages have only recently received electricity. All roads were in a deplorable condition. Most places did not have regular supply of drinking water. Since the region has sufficient rainfall, simple rain harvesting methods were used to store drinking water. Some people were aware of water contamination due to coal mining. On a few rooftops there were receivers for television (DTH) and almost everyone owned a mobile while poverty levels hovered around 40%.

The availability of a range of options to choose from remains a distant dream for the general population. There are a few schools up to the 10th standard, but most were below Class 8. Several schools have been initiated and being managed by missionaries to impart education and improve literacy rates. From feedback received, it appears that the present young generation of these areas seemed uninterested in education. The income generated from coal mining and its distribution remains highly skewed. Income and wealth disparities have only widened over the years. In a recent news item in the local daily[14], a top police official said that a number of people including traders, businessmen and Rangbah Shnongs could be arrested for their links with the militant outfit HNLC who were carrying out extortion in Jaintia Hills. Many of those people with such links with the rebel group were from Khliehriat, Lad Rymbai and villages on the Indo-Bangladesh border. Some have already been booked under the Unlawful Activities Prevention Act.

14. *The Shillong Times*, April 7, 2008.

In summary, the State in general and Jaintia Hills in particular have been experiencing massive economic losses as huge volumes of coal are extracted and sent out of the State. With the establishment of Cement Manufacturing Company Ltd (CMCL) (Star Cement), local suppliers from Lumshnong have been supplying coal, limestone, sand, etc.[15] The suppliers now allege that they have been exploited as the rates for their materials are below the market rates. However, these enterprises have also failed to create employment opportunities for the local people. The influx of a large unrecorded population has already changed the demographic profile of the region though officials do not reveal it.

c) Areas of Concern: Health and Environment

The rampant and unscientific coal mining in this unorganised sector has led to serious environmental disasters. Very little is known about the health status of workers who have migrated from other regions and swamped the area. For the sake of profits, health and safety norms have been neglected. Mine owners do not care about their employees as well as the environment. Accidents and fatalities remain unreported and whether compensation is given is also unknown. In the words of a manager, 'the owner doesn't care about maintenance or workers; all he cares about is money'. In the absence of laws, workers and the environment will continue to be mercilessly exploited.

Large volumes of timber trade from the region, in the past, had considerably reduced the forest cover to less than 40% in the area. At present, the rapid expansion of coal trade and coal stockpiling has led to serious ecological problems. The scale of environmental degradation in the coal mining areas of Jaintia Hills District has been so immense that it prompted a study by the Meghalaya State Pollution Control Board. In its 1997 report 'Environmental Impact of Coal

15. *The Shillong Times*, May 5, 2008.

Mining in Jaintia Hills', it mentioned that the most significant impacts were on land use, water quality, air quality, ecological and socio-economic aspects. Detailed investigations were carried out in two vital areas examining the status of (i) surface and ground water and (ii) ambient air quality. The study concluded that the coal mining operations had adversely affected the quality of water that rivers, streams and groundwater have turned highly acidic. Rivers and streams had become totally unfit for fisheries and aquatic life. The air quality of the coal mining areas, which fall under residential, rural and other areas as per the national ambient air quality standard, too had degraded to a certain extent. In the last 11 years since the report, further degradation has taken place in the absence of mining laws. The State's mining policy is still at the draft stage.

6

Conclusion

The total cropped area in Jaintia Hills District is only 9% and taking into account other areas such as forests, as much as 50% of Jaintia Hills is not available for cultivation. With the rapid pace of environmental deterioration, even lesser land would be available for cultivation in the future. Vast areas may become uninhabitable and uncultivable due to water contamination. At present, there is neither any data available on the area of land lost to mining in the State nor any report of any displacement. The workers' working conditions covering aspects of safety and health are ignored by mine owners. Incidents of accidents and lives lost are unreported. There is no known instance of any struggle for workers' rights. While the coal mine owners association represents a strong lobby having considerable influence on regional politics, the workers on the other hand, remain disorganised and exploited. No study has so far examined the socio–economic status of those involved with mining.

With mining not under the ambit of any law, few individuals continue to reap the benefits at the cost of others and utter disregard for the environment. Being in the unorganised sector, government offices and officials cannot give out much information other than the ones obtained under royalty collection and cess imposed. Thus the mines are at a perilous state that only time and tide will force government to intervene, be it with the environmental laws or labour laws or any other laws. Mining operations lack scientific methods and follow the most rudimentary method of mining. The mining areas in forest and agricultural lands are destroying the ecosystem and the rich biodiversity and land reclamation may be impossible.

It is often said that mining has not brought development to the region and the state. The benefits are often construed to be reaped by few individuals. It can be seen that in mining areas like Lad Rymbai, Bapung, Khliehriat, which have been mining for the last thirty years, have not seen much sign of economic and social progress. The living standards of the vast majority remain pitiful. The availability of electricity, conditions of roads, institutions like schools, health centres, etc. remain deplorable.

There is not much value addition to the minerals extracted except for limestone, and this has led to huge economic losses for the State. Most Industrial units of the State are not resource based. Besides, unregulated mining has led to influx of outside communities of unidentified antecedents. The demographic changes are imminent with a large ghost population.

The mining of uranium is still debated upon. The DAE is hopeful of uranium mining in Meghalaya[16] while pressure groups continue to oppose. The Khasi Hills Autonomous District Council (KHADC) has been asked not to renew the NOC[17] due to health hazards, influx and land alienation. As noted columnist P. Mukhim once quoted, 'Delhi does not seem to bother about these *minor* details since the motto is to *exploit* all available resources to feed the ever growing demand of industry. The question is whether India's north-east can make that ultimate sacrifice of becoming the powerhouse of the nation at the cost of its own threatened

16. *The Shillong Times*, April 22, 2008.
17. *The Shillong Times*, May 7, 2008.

existence?' The Draft Mining Policy of the State is yet to be implemented. One hopes for sincere efforts from people at the helm of affairs to make responsible decisions, NGOs to aid, assist and check the present crossroads the State finds itself in and peoples movements to initiate changes.

References

1. Chattopathyay, S.K.*Tribal Institutions of Meghalaya*, Spectrum Publications, Guwahati, 1985.
2. Directorate of Mineral Resources, Government of Meghalaya.
3. Dutta, B.B. *Land Relations in North East India*, People's Publishing House, New Delhi, 1987.
4. Dutta Ray, B. (ed.) *Population, Poverty and Environment in North East India*, Concept Publishing Company, New Delhi, 2000.
5. Dutta, R. "Coal Export from Meghalaya to Bangladesh: A Case Study of the Borsora Trade Route" in Das, Gurudas and R.K. Purkayastha (eds.), *Border-Trade: North East India and Neighbouring Countries*, Akansha Publishing House, New Delhi, 2000.
6. Dutta, R. "Structural Change and Strategy of Development: Resource Industry Linkages in Meghalaya" in Das, Gurudas (ed.), *Structural Change and Strategy of Development: Resource Industry Linkages in North East India,* Akansha Publishing House, New Delhi, 2005.
7. Meghalaya State Pollution Control Board, *Environmental Impact of Coal Mining in Jaintia Hills District*, 1997.
8. *Primary Census Abstract*, Census of India, 2001
9. *Report on Fourth Economic Census, Meghalaya, Part I & II*, Directorate of Economics and Statistics, Government of Meghalaya, 1998.
10. Rymbai, R.T. *Shillong and its Land System*, Shillong Centenary Souvenir, 1976, pp. 29-30.
11. Sarma, S. *Meghalaya: Land and Forest*, Geophil Publishing House, Guwahati, 2003.

12. *Statistical Hand Book,* Meghalaya, Directorate of Economics and Statistics, Government of Meghalaya, Various issues.
13. *The Shillong Times.*
14. www.nedfi.com: NE Data Bank.
15. http://saipdata.awardspace.com/

Annexure

Health and Environmental Hazards

Technically environmental and health factors are interlinked. During our interactions with the people, it was suggested that normally workers are not concerned about either their own health or of their surroundings. For them chronic cough is not due to gas build up, fatigue is not caused by extremely poor working conditions, polluted or rather acidified water is not caused by the dumping of coal but they are all just another normal thing. The methodology of work is downright primitive. The consequences are death from 'caving in of mines', flooding of mines in rainy season, plots of residential areas and sometimes roads caving in etc.

The normal process is for miners to dig 90 ft to 140 ft straight down depending on the availability of resources, and then when the assumed safe depth is reached, choose a direction and then charge forward till wherever possible. During this process of 'rat mining' they dig under areas that are residential areas or even roads and highways. There have been several cases of houses suddenly disappearing into the ground below or people dying because the road gave way to the caves below while they were driving. There is a story shared by a few inhabitants about the cruelty of mine owners and the politics that they play—*An excavation was underway and miners wanted to pass through an area where a church was situated. The priest resisted. The mine owner brought in police. They led the priest just past a hill and shot him dead, because he was meddling in the miners' affairs.*

Here are some pictures taken during the simple trekking in Jaiñtia Hills.

1. A typical mining area: There are no planned roads to enter this area. Where ever the 'Shaktimaan truck' can manoeuvre forms the road. Workers in this area chase away any kind of information seekers especially after the Public Interest Litigation that was launched against mining. The hut just near the mine is a place for mending tools, etc. usually done by elderly workers. The huts to the side are the houses for the workers. These houses are common sightings in mining areas. The box that you see is the measuring tool for measuring the amount of coal brought out in a day.

Maintenance work being undertaken in a mine. That's how you can get into a mine. Cut several trees, project them at an angle, and add steps to finish. We were told the initial bridge was weak and collapsed. Fortunately no one was working

at that time. We met the 'sordar' while he was doing the maintenance work. He said 'the owner doesn't care about maintenance or workers; all he cares about is money'. This pit was 110 feet deep, so you can imagine working in dim light, gas buildup, claustrophobia and overall uncertainty of being safe.

Children playing near coal pits. This is a common sight near coal mines, in depots or on the roadside. They have no worry about cleanliness, education, etc. They are cautioned about talking to strangers or 'people with cameras'.

Enroute to villages beyond Lad Rymbai (Mine rich area).

A stock or a (depot) 'diphu'

A typical loading from 'diphu' (depot)

Plot of greenery turned barren

A very deep perilous mine

A very deep perilous mine

Water logged mines, a common phenomenon during autumn

What is their future goal?

Going to school on a chilly morning